W
A

David Winter

A LION POCKETBOOK
Oxford · Batavia · Sydney

Text copyright © 1991 David Winter
This edition copyright © 1991 Lion Publishing

Published by
Lion Publishing plc
Sandy Lane West, Oxford, England
ISBN 0 7459 2137 X
Lion Publishing Corporation
1705 Hubbard Avenue, Batavia, Illinois 60510, USA
ISBN 0 7459 2137 X
Albatross Books Pty Ltd
PO Box 320, Sutherland, NSW 2232, Australia
ISN 0 7324 0496 7

First edition 1991

Printed and bound in Yugoslavia

Contents

1

Birth and death

There are only two things that are certain to happen in any life. One is birth. The other is death.

We celebrate the birth of a baby—it's a champagne occasion, with congratulations all round. But a death is an occasion for sympathy, condolences and hushed voices. There could hardly be a bigger contrast.

We describe the mother approaching childbirth as 'expectant'—she's looking forward eagerly to the event. But hardly anyone looks forward to death. It's something to be put off as long as possible.

We spend a great deal of time thinking about and planning for a birth, but we would think it morbid for people to prepare or plan for death. So we approach the two unavoidable events in our lives in totally contrasted ways. Indeed, if it were possible we'd prefer never to think about death at all.

Yet there it is, like a dark, solid wall crossing the

path of our lives, totally unavoidable and inevitable. Sooner or later, because of our own old age or illness, or that of someone we love, we shall be forced to face that reality. That's when the questions come thick and fast—and that's when we realize how little we have really thought about it or know about it.

Because I wrote a little book on life beyond death over twenty years ago I've often been asked to speak

Everyone has to die. But is there a way through to a life beyond?

or broadcast on the subject—not because I'm an 'expert' but because I've actually dared to go public on such a hush-hush subject.

Among the broadcasts have been a number of phone-in programmes. There I've been bombarded with difficult (and sometimes unanswerable) questions on life after death. From those programmes I've compiled a list of the dozen or so most frequent questions which people ask. In this book I've set out my answers to them.

In a way, they're not my answers, because as far as I can I've tried to give straightforward answers from the Bible. I have tried as far as possible to tell people what the Christian faith has to say on the subject rather than what I have worked out for myself. So these answers are not so much my ideas or opinions as a broad summary of what the Christian church has taught for nearly two thousand years.

Some of these questions are profound and get right to the heart of our human meaning and existence. Others may seem a bit trivial or even ludicrous ('Will there be dogs in heaven?')—but they aren't trivial to those who ask them.

Perhaps more than anything, these questions show how much people want to believe in life after death yet can't imagine it as anything more than a better version of this life—a sort of second innings, on a better wicket. I suppose it's not surprising that we find it hard to consider a totally different dimension of existence. Our questions, and the Bible's answers, may help to stretch our thinking a bit. At any rate, I hope they will increase our faith.

2

Wishful thinking?

**Is there really anything beyond death?
Isn't it just wishful thinking?**

I visited a woman in my parish whose husband was
dying of cancer. I sat there rather awkwardly,
wondering if and how I could tactfully introduce a
religious dimension into a conversation about
doctors, treatment and the problems of getting in to
the city hospital during the rush hour. She was not a
church-goer. Indeed, she had let me know that while
her husband was, in her words, a 'Christian', she was
not a believer of any kind. Yet suddenly, abruptly,
she fired a question at me.

'Do you believe in life after death?'

Before I could begin a reply, she added, 'No,
really.'

The question said it all, and it's one that I've
frequently faced in debates and broadcasts—though
seldom as painfully or directly as in that woman's
sitting-room.

I was there as an official spokesman for a religion

We long for a bridge between life on earth and life with God.

that has as a central belief the assertion that its founder rose from the dead and that through him people can have what the Bible calls 'eternal life'. But is it true? And—more directly—did even I believe it? Or was the whole thing a monstrous confidence trick, a sop to people's fear of death, a way of cushioning the pain of bereavement? Did I really believe it . . . not just as an article of the faith, but as part of the truth of our existence: the way things actually are? Can human beings really live on beyond the traumatic and apparently final experience which we call death?

We talk about a 'terminal' illness. Well, we all know that the terminus is the end of the line, the place where everything stops. Can we believe that beyond this 'terminus' there is somewhere else to go, some more travelling to be done?

The first thing to say, of course, is that in the nature of things such a belief can never be proved absolutely. Death removes people from this sphere of existence. There's no point in denying that. They are no longer available as witnesses to what may happen on the other side of death.

There has, though, been one such witness, Christians believe. And it is to the experience of Jesus Christ that I would always turn in any serious attempt to answer this question. He died. Beyond any reasonable doubt, Jesus the prophet from Nazareth was put to death, probably in the year 30AD.

Yet his friends were absolutely convinced that on

the third day after his execution he 'rose from the dead'. His tomb was found to be empty and he appeared to them on a number of occasions—not as a ghost or apparition, but as a whole person: body, mind and spirit, as we would say.

These 'appearances', recorded in the Gospels, make fascinating reading. Some were to individuals, such as Mary Magdalene. Some were to small groups of people—two, three or four at a time. Some were to larger groups—even, according to the apostle Paul, as many as five hundred people at once. If those were hallucinations, then they were hallucinations on the grand scale!

As a result of these appearances the followers of Jesus became convinced that he was alive. In fact, they were so convinced that most of them were prepared to suffer torture and even death rather than deny it.

It is a matter of historical record that within about forty years the new religion of Christianity, based entirely on the belief that Jesus Christ rose from the dead, was believed and being promoted throughout the whole Roman Empire.

The authorities detested the new religion and did all they could to wipe it out. Obviously the best way to have done that would have been to prove that Jesus did not rise from the dead. It shouldn't have been very difficult, yet they failed to do it. Indeed, as far as we can discover, they made no serious attempt to counter this apparently incredible claim. The Christian Church continued to grow, openly preaching that Jesus rose from the dead, and within a couple of centuries Christianity became the official religion of the Roman Empire.

Now the importance of all this in answering the question 'Is there really life beyond death?' is that it actually provides some evidence on the subject—something well beyond wishful thinking. People can look at the accounts of the death and resurrection of Jesus and decide whether they find them convincing or not. My experience is that when people look at them in an unprejudiced way they do find them convincing—and that these accounts tell them fascinating things about the nature of life after death . . . but more of that later.

For now, let me just say that the resurrection of Jesus is the best evidence we have that there is life beyond death. It isn't the only evidence, by any means, but most of the rest lies in the field of psychic research and personal testimony—near-death experiences, apparitions and the like. It is sketchy and at times contradictory, but taken together it is an impressive body of evidence that there is more to all this than meets the modern sceptical eye.

Not only that, but every human civilization that we know of has had a belief in life after death in some form or other. It may be the Elysian Fields of the Romans, the Valhalla of the Norsemen or the Happy Hunting Grounds of the American Indians, but the universal instinct of the human race has always been that death is not the end.

We may choose to call it wishful thinking, or the

product of a fear of death. But it's surprising that such beliefs should have persisted right through the history of our race up to and including the modern scientific age, if there is no reality behind them.

For me, Jesus Christ remains the outstanding witness to that reality. However we read the Gospel accounts—and they are not quite as straightforward as they may seem at first glance—they offer us evidence from a group of reliable, honest and courageous people who were convinced that they had met someone who had been fully dead and was now fully alive.

We shouldn't be put off by claims that those first Christians lived in a gullible age. They didn't. Most of their contemporaries were as sceptical about the idea of someone rising from the dead as any modern people.

Neither should we worry that their eyewitness testimony had been distorted or exaggerated by the time it reached the pages of the Gospels. After all, most of those same witnesses—as the apostle Paul pointed out to some doubting Christians at Corinth—were still around when the earlier Gospels were being written.

'Why should it seem so incredible that God should raise the dead?' That was a question Paul put to the judge at his trial. It's a good question. God created life itself. Christians believe that he has also created eternal life—life with him beyond death—for those who trust him on this side of it.

3

In touch with the dead?

**Can we get in touch with those who have died?
Can we pray for them?**

For years the Spiritualists had a slogan which often
appeared on notice boards outside their meeting
halls: 'All religions preach survival; only spiritual-
ism proves it.'

Over the years I've been surprised at how many
bereaved people, including many with a strong
Christian faith, pay at least one visit to a spiritualist
seance. When asked why, most say that at that point
they were prepared to do anything to get in touch
with their loved one. Some hoped that it would be
like talking to them on the phone when they were
away in another country on a business trip.

In the event, most found it a disappointing
experience and did not go back. A few persisted for a
while, hoping in the end for something more
substantial than the irrelevant 'messages' (often
concerned with trivial details of the past rather than
the present) that seemed to be all that came from the

'other side'. And a very few became hooked on a regular diet of seances, finding some kind of satisfaction in the experience but often, and sadly, failing to come to terms with the reality of their bereavement.

So what is the answer to the question, 'Can we get in touch with those who have died?' Spiritualists will say 'yes' we can, and we should. Followers of other religions, especially Jews and Christians, will say that it may be possible, in some circumstances, to communicate with those who have died, but that we shouldn't do it—indeed, that the practice is directly forbidden by God in the Bible. And many bereavement counsellors, religious and secular, would say that attempting to contact the dead by psychic or occult means is psychologically dangerous and emotionally unsatisfying.

The only clear example in the Bible of this practice is the story of King Saul and the witch of Endor. She was a famous medium, and King Saul persuaded her to conjure up the spirit of the prophet Samuel, who had died some time previously. He hoped that Samuel would give him some good advice. He got some 'advice', but it wasn't what he wanted to hear and the whole episode ended in tragedy. What the Bible makes clear in this story is that Saul was tampering with things in a realm that he had no right to enter. It was forbidden territory.

So my answer to the first part of this question is, 'Perhaps we can, but no, we shouldn't.'

That brings us to the second part, about praying

Some people claim special powers to make contact beyond the grave.

for those who have died.

I have to admit that Christians are divided over this. They all agree that it is right and proper to remember those who have died in our prayers and to thank God for them.

Some Christians wish to go further, and ask that God would complete his purpose for them, or that they might enjoy perpetual light and peace in God's presence. Others feel that to pray in this way is to imply that heaven is not perfect or that something more remains to be done than Jesus Christ has already done by dying for them.

It's not a difference that need trouble us too much. Whenever we pray, we acknowledge that what really matters is God's will. We don't pray to try to make him change his mind! Prayer is co-operating with God in his purpose, and we don't have to spell out to him in our prayers what we think that is. Indeed, sometimes we can't possibly know.

So it seems to me perfectly natural for a bereaved person to pray about the one they have lost. It would be unnatural if suddenly, at the moment of their death, they were to be wiped out of our prayers.

The simplest thing to do is what we should always do in our prayers: tell God honestly and frankly what is on our hearts and then leave it to him to do what is best. That is why we pray, 'Your will, not mine, be done.' God knows what is best for our loved ones and for ourselves. To pray rightly is to recognize that and to trust him completely.

4

A new body

**Do Christians believe that dead bodies rise up
from their graves? If so, what about people who
are cremated?**

The short answer is: No, they don't. Christians
believe in resurrection, which is a very different
matter.

There's a cartoon in a book called *Sacred and
Confidential* which shows two monks looking at a
huge stone tomb in a cathedral. One is saying to the
other, 'Imagine resurrecting through that lot!'

In fact, as I hope the monk knows, we don't
'resurrect' through things at all. Our old body
disintegrates and God gives us a new, resurrection
body. That's what the New Testament tells us, and
that's what happened, uniquely, to Jesus.

About twenty years after the first Easter the
apostle Paul was writing to the Christians at Corinth
to tell them that 'flesh and blood'—in other words,
ordinary human bodies—simply cannot go on into
the kingdom of heaven. And common sense
endorses that. These bodies of ours are very well

adapted to life on this planet, but even a relatively short-range trip outside its atmosphere and gravity creates enormous problems.

Whatever 'heaven' is, it's certainly not on this planet! So to live in heaven we need new 'bodies', bodies designed by God for life in a completely new environment.

Jesus said that we need to be 'born again' to enter the kingdom of heaven—we need a totally new life for a new sphere of living. He wasn't only talking about life after death, of course, but of life in the new community which he came to found.

But life in that community isn't limited to this world—that's why it's the kingdom of heaven as well as the kingdom of God. 'Resurrection' is the way in which God changes us, giving us new bodies as well as new minds and spirits with which to live in his new world.

The Bible compares this resurrection to a growing seed being 'clothed' with its own appropriate plant-form. A cabbage seed produces a cabbage, but the final product doesn't look a bit like the seed from which it has grown. Our 'resurrection' bodies develop from the 'seed' of what we are now, but what God makes of it is infinitely more wonderful.

You can see this in the resurrection of Jesus. Before his death and burial he had a completely normal human body. If he wanted to go somewhere, he had to walk or ride. If he didn't eat he was hungry. If you crucified him, he died.

But after his resurrection there was obviously a great change in his body. He appeared in locked rooms and at different locations many miles apart. He was not a ghost, he told his followers, but he was clearly not a 'normal' human being either. In fact, on most of the occasions when he appeared to them they didn't recognize him at first, though later they were absolutely convinced that it was him.

All of this seems consistent with the Christian belief that after death our earthly bodies disintegrate ('Dust to dust, ashes to ashes,' as we say in the funeral service), and God provides for us a new, resurrection body, no longer shackled to space and time, no longer subject to decay, pain and death—a body designed for heaven.

So it doesn't make any difference how our earthly body comes to its disintegration. Some are buried. Some are cremated. Some people are blown up in an explosion or drowned at sea. It makes no difference to God and it shouldn't matter to us.

What does matter is that my spirit—the real 'me'—as it returns to God should know him and trust him. Because it is faith and trust in God that opens up a whole new way of living after this earthly life is ended, in a completely new environment which the Bible calls 'heaven'.

Our bodies will lie in the grave, but the New Testament speaks of new 'bodies' beyond death.

5

How can we know anything?

How can we know anything for sure about life beyond the grave, seeing no one can come back to tell us about it?

I'm told that the baby in the womb is very apprehensive about being born. The womb is familiar, warm and secure. Food is regular and reliable. There is no harsh noise, just the steady throbbing of mother's heart. There is that gentle fluid in which to float.

Who in their senses would exchange that comfortable existence for life in the world outside? There, harsh lights shine, there is noise, shock, pain and danger. No wonder the baby recoils from birth and no wonder its trauma leaves its mark on all of us.

But looking back, from our experience of life, would any sane person really want to go back into the womb and stay there? Through the shock and trauma of birth the baby enters a whole new world of interest, excitement and possibilities—a world it couldn't possibly have imagined, utterly different from life in the womb in almost every way. But only by being born can it find out. There are no messages from the outside world to the unborn baby.

Now if that is true of birth, which marks the start of earthly life, why shouldn't it also be true of death, which marks its end?

Like the baby in the womb, we fear the unknown. We cling to the present. Even if our life is hard, at least it is familiar. Beyond death lies ... well, what? Light, shock, growth, possibilities, new relationships? Only by going through death can we ever find out. But, like the baby, we may well discover that what we feared is far better than what we have now.

And, of course, it isn't totally unknown. As we have seen already, Jesus has been there for us. In the words of the Bible, 'he has tasted death for everyone'. On our behalf he has gone through the veil into the next world and come back to show us that it is not miserable but marvellous.

When the apostle Paul was expecting at any moment to be put to death, he wrote to his friends at Philippi saying that he longed 'to be with Christ, which is far better'. 'Far better' than what? Than house arrest? Well yes, of course. Than his earlier life of adventure and influence? Yes, that as well. But I think he meant far better than any life he had ever known, because he had just written in the same letter that for him 'to live is Christ, and to die is gain'.

Not many of us, probably, could be quite so confident. Yet it was the experience of meeting the risen Jesus on the road to Damascus that gave Paul his confidence, and that experience can also be ours—not on the road to Damascus, but wherever we are.

The many biblical pictures of heaven can be summed up in the one thought: there is life on the other side of death.

6

What about animals?

Are there animals in heaven? It wouldn't be heaven to me if my dog weren't there.

I don't suppose the person asking this question is very bothered about the presence of man-eating tigers, alligators or pythons in heaven. They are concerned about a particular animal that was very important to them—a dog, in this case, but it might just as easily have been a cat or even a budgerigar.

Human beings sometimes, for complicated reasons, find it easier to relate to a pet than to other people. So it isn't surprising that for such a person heaven couldn't possibly be perfect in the absence of their pet.

Animals as pets weren't a big part of life in Bible times, so this isn't a question to which the Bible addresses itself. There is no mention of animals in the visions of heaven in Revelation.

But what can be said is that heaven is the place where all the deficiencies, inadequacies and failures of earth will be put right . . . and that must include any inadequacies or imperfections in our relationships, with people and with the rest of creation. We shall be at one with our Creator and with all that he has created.

I don't know whether there will be dogs in heaven, but I am absolutely sure that in God's kingdom of perfect love there will be no feelings of loss or deprivation. Because if there were (to quote the question) 'it wouldn't be heaven'.

7

Marriage in heaven

Will we recognize other people in heaven? And will we still have the same relationships and ties as we had on earth?

I'm sure that the answer to the first part of the question is 'yes'. When Jesus appeared to his disciples in his resurrection form they recognized him. They didn't always do so at once and sometimes they seemed to recognize him not through his appearance but through his voice, actions or mannerisms. But what matters is that they were left in no doubt that it was him—Jesus, their teacher and friend.

Perhaps his appearance was changed in some way. Those who have had some physical handicap or disability on earth would not expect it to be continued in heaven. Those who have taken part in the resurrection are no longer mortal. In the words of Jesus, 'They can no longer die'. But, however different Jesus looked, the disciples 'knew it was the Lord'—and were utterly and permanently sure of it.

So I think we can safely assume that we shall

recognize one another in heaven.

The second part of the question is more complicated, because there lies behind it just a hint of that possessiveness that marks—and often spoils—human relationships.

'I want you all to myself' is a frequent expression of human love, but in terms of the perfect community of heaven it is very excluding. After all, many people have never had access to one of these satisfyingly exclusive relationships. Are they to be 'deprived' for eternity?

Jesus was once asked a trick question about marriages in heaven. If a woman during her lifetime were married to seven different men—being widowed by each of them—whose wife would she be 'at the resurrection'?

He declined to answer the question, which he said related to 'the people of this age', who 'marry and are given in marriage'. He went on: 'Those who are considered worthy of taking part in that age and in the resurrection from the dead will neither marry nor be given in marriage, and they can no longer die; for they are like the angels. They are God's children, since they are children of the resurrection.'

What are we to make of this? Not, I think, that relationships on earth will be wiped out in heaven. That would be a contradiction of love. But there will

Old age can sometimes bring loneliness, and a longing to be reunited with those we have loved.

be no new exclusive relationships—no 'marrying and giving in marriage'—and the principal relationship of all of us will be found in that simple phrase: 'they are God's children'.

Our relationship with him will transform, purify and perfect all our other relationships. We won't want to keep people to ourselves, but see them all as our brothers and sisters, close to one another because we are all now close to God.

8

What about hell?

What about hell? If my husband has gone to hell I don't want to go to heaven. Is hell a place? And who goes there? How could a loving God send anyone into everlasting torment?

Let's assume that we live in a world created by a good God. Now look around you. Does it look like it? All around us there are big wars and small riots, crime, violence, dishonesty, cruelty and injustice. Evil people peddle drugs, making themselves a fortune by destroying the lives of others. Lies are told. Innocent men and women find their lives ruined by the greed and cruelty of the powerful.

And evil people get away with it! Tyrants die in their beds, while their victims die in foul prisons.

For a world allegedly created by a good God— called by the Bible 'the judge of all the earth'—it all looks pretty unimpressive. Is God unable to do anything about it, or unwilling? If he's unable, then he isn't all-powerful, as the Bible says he is. If he's unwilling, then, quite frankly, he's not a good God at all.

The truth is, if this life is all there is, then God

would be shown to be either powerless to put right wrongs, or unwilling to do it.

Both ideas are unthinkable for those who believe in God. As we have seen, this life is not 'all there is'. Indeed, most of the world's other faiths, as well as Christianity, hold to the belief that there is a judgment of our life's actions beyond death. God does not sit by idly while evil rules in the world he has created.

All our actions—indeed, our words and motives, too—are the raw material of a judgment that awaits us. It is a judgment in which we unconsciously write the verdict ourselves: it is what we do with our lives now that determines what happens to us later.

Without such an idea of judgment—yes, and retribution or punishment—beyond death, this would in fact be a world of almost total injustice.

The distinctive thing about the Christian notion of judgment, however, is that God actually wants to spare people the consequences of their wrong-doing. He has done something about it by sending his Son, Jesus, so that 'whoever believes in him will not perish, but have eternal life'.

Hell is a reality rather than a place. Those who reject God and his morality have cut themselves off from all that is good, loving and true. I suppose it is a 'place' in a negative sense: it's where God isn't.

But it isn't God's purpose that any human being should end up in hell. 'He is not willing that any should perish,' says the Bible, 'but that all should come to repentance.' In fact, the only beings who are actually described as consigned to hell in the Bible are 'the devil and his angels'—those evil forces and powers that have spoilt God's perfect world.

Of course, if people use their God-given free will to follow those evil forces and reject God's offer of forgiveness, then it may well be that they will share their fate. But if they do it won't be God's choice, but theirs.

From all this you will see that these questions can't be answered in stark, categorical terms. No one but God knows who has accepted his offer and who has rejected it. Some people leave it very late—yes, even to their deathbed. But only God can possibly know the destiny of any human spirit, and we are acting God if we start declaring who is, and who is not, acceptable to him.

What we do know is that his love and mercy far exceed ours. His love has gone to the greatest possible lengths to reach out to us—even to the length of giving his Son to die for us. His mercy is without limits.

So when we think of our loved ones who have died, especially those who seemed to us to have had little or no faith in God, we should be slow to jump to the conclusion that he has rejected them.

As a minister I have often found more faith, perhaps especially during a time of illness or weakness, than a person's nearest or dearest would have expected. God looks for evidence of faith, it's true—but Jesus spoke of faith 'like a grain of mustard seed' . . . something quite tiny at present but capable of growth. God is not looking for reasons to reject us, but for grounds to draw us into his kingdom.

So I think it is right to be positive and optimistic rather than negative and defeatist about our loved ones who have died. We can be absolutely sure that God will deal with them justly and mercifully. As the Bible says, 'God did not send his Son into the world to condemn the world, but that the world through him might be saved.'

9

Life to the full

If heaven is supposed to be so marvellous, why are Christians so reluctant to push off and go there? Surely a real Christian would actually want to be there?

I don't see anything contradictory about looking forward to heaven but enjoying life now. The alternative would be to become obsessed with what lies beyond the grave while neglecting our responsibilities and opportunities here on earth—which is almost exactly what Lenin accused Christians of doing!

In fact, God wants us to live life here and now to the full, to our maximum potential. At the same time we should always remember that this life is not the end and that one day we will answer to God for our behaviour on earth.

Of course, there is a difference between death and dying. I have sat with terminally ill patients for whom death itself has no terrors, but the prospect of going through the process of dying fills them with alarm. That is perfectly understandable. Death is a state. Dying is an event.

Being married is a state, and the bride and groom look forward to that. But a wedding is an event, and they may well be scared stiff at the prospect. That doesn't mean that they don't want to get married!

The state of death offers us at the least an end to pain. The event of dying may involve us in discomfort, distress and indignity. In fact, in the modern world it should normally involve none of those things, but the prospect of it isn't appealing, however strong our faith.

The apostle Paul, facing the prospect of death, said that he was in two minds: whether he wished to stay in his present body and continue his fruitful work, or 'to depart and be with Christ, which is better by far'.

I dare say many Christians have felt that same inner conflict. It is neither cowardice nor lack of faith that leads them to decide, as Paul did, that they should stay where God has put them, doing what he has called them to do, until the moment when he decides that they should move on.

Even if we live life to our full potential, we still yearn for a greater fulfilment hereafter.

10

Who goes to heaven?

**Who decides whether or not we go to heaven?
Is there really a gate where St Peter sits, letting
some in and keeping some out? If so, what are
the tests he uses?**

No, there isn't a gate with St Peter sitting at it. The
idea comes from some words of Jesus, when he told
the apostle Peter that he would have 'the keys of the
kingdom of heaven' with the authority to 'bind and
loose' things in earth and in heaven. But I don't
think any biblical expert thinks that those words
mean Peter was given the job of pearly gate
receptionist.

Peter was instrumental in spreading the good
news about Jesus. You could say he opened the
kingdom of heaven to the Jews when he preached
about Jesus on the day of Pentecost, recorded in the
Acts of the Apostles. Then, a few years later, he
opened the kingdom of heaven to Gentiles when he
explained the same message to a Roman officer and
his household, and then baptized them. This is also
recorded in Acts.

However, the message he preached sets out what

the question above calls the 'tests' for entrance into eternal life. The New Testament puts it like this: 'This is the message. God has given us life, and that life is in his Son. Those who have the Son have life. Those who do not have the Son of God do not have life.' Or, in even better known words, 'God so loved the world that he gave his only Son, so that whoever believes in him should not perish, but have eternal life.'

It is really as simple as that. Eternal life is a gift from God, and the key that releases it to us is faith.

Of course, if someone has never heard of Jesus they can't be expected to put their faith in him. For such people a merciful God judges them according to the way they have followed their consciences and obeyed what the Bible calls the 'natural law'. You can read about that in Paul's letter to the Romans, chapter 2.

As I have said before, God doesn't lightly exclude anyone. 'He is not willing that any should perish,' says the Bible. The gates of heaven are never closed but, sadly, there are people who obstinately refuse to enter them. The fact is, though, that anyone who ends up outside will be there by their own choice, not God's.

11

Will we enjoy heaven?

I simply can't visualize a life beyond this one—and I can't believe it will be better. Who wants to be a wispy ghost or a kind of angel? I'd sooner settle for extinction.

Yes, so would I. But that's not the choice. For one thing, extinction would make judgment after death pointless, wouldn't it—and leave evil unpunished and wrongs unrighted.

For another, we aren't going to be 'wispy ghosts'—or angels, for that matter—in heaven. The risen Jesus wasn't a 'wispy ghost' but a complete person, who could talk to his friends, share a meal with them and even join them on a night-time fishing expedition.

No one in their right mind would want to be a ghost, existing in some kind of twilight half-world between dream and reality. Extinction would indeed be preferable. But the kind of eternal life God offers is nothing like that, and the risen Jesus is the evidence.

Still, I do agree that it is impossible to visualize life beyond death, if by that you mean having clear-cut and detailed ideas about what it will be like.

But we can 'visualize' in another sense—we can share in the visions of heaven provided for us by the book of Revelation in the Bible. These are not detailed accounts of future events but pictures—visions—of what is humanly speaking indescribable. But we are entitled to use them to inspire our imagination and strengthen our faith.

Surely a state of perfect peace, healing and love which the book of Revelation describes is 'better' than this life? A society where the great powers lay down their sovereignty at God's feet, where the ancient rivalries of tribes, nations and cultures are healed for ever, where there is no more bereavement, pain or suffering... isn't that preferable to any human society we have ever known?

God created a very beautiful planet for us—which we have spoiled—and the lovely experience of human love, which we have often abused. Clearly he makes nice things! Can't we believe that his final triumph will be to re-create a world where beauty and love will be unspoiled? Heaven will be God's demonstration of what life is like without sin.

The fact that you and I can't 'visualize' it is neither here nor there. I can't 'visualize' the creation of matter, or the infinite power locked into a single atom—but they are real. It's not for us to put limits on what God can do.

12

Reincarnation or resurrection?

I find the idea of reincarnation more logical and convincing than the Christian idea of resurrection. How do we know the Hindus aren't right, and Christians wrong?

Let's deal with the first part first. Personally I don't find the Hindu concept of reincarnation (or the 'transmigration of souls') in the least bit logical or convincing. For one thing, it assumes a fixed number of 'souls', endlessly moving up and down the scale of worthiness. I doubt whether that can be defended logically in a world where the human population, certainly, has multiplied enormously in the last century.

The attraction of reincarnation is that it seems to give us an infinite number of chances to get things right, whereas the Christian doctrine is a bit more stark: 'it is appointed to man to die once, and after that comes judgment.' There is no notion in Christian belief of hundreds, thousands or even millions of chances to get it right. We have one life, one death and one judgment.

So perhaps it's not so much that reincarnation is

more logical, but that it's more attractive. It removes any concept of ultimate judgment and asks us to believe that in the end even the most dilatory may achieve improvement, and perhaps one day union with the Infinite.

But does it simply come down to which belief we find more logical or more attractive? In fact, it is impossible to rationalize such subjects, because they are literally beyond us. We can't know about life beyond death, because we haven't been there. We can't say one view seems right and another wrong. All we can really say is, 'God only knows'.

He does, and he has told us. That is the Christian claim. He hasn't left us in the dark to work it out for ourselves. He has revealed the truth to us—and when you think about it, there's no other way in which we can possibly know the truth for sure. God knows . . . and he has shown us, not all there is to know, but all we need to know about life beyond death.

That 'revelation' is through his Son, Jesus. He was the perfect expression on earth of God's truth. What he has said and what he taught his followers is all we need to know.

And what has he said? That eternal life is God's gift to those who believe in his Son. Not extinction at the moment of death and not an endless series of reincarnations, but resurrection into a new world, a new existence . . . God's new society, the kingdom of heaven.

13

What is heaven like?

What is heaven like? Sitting around playing harps for all eternity sounds pretty boring. Will there be things to do?

The Bible tells us that heaven is better than our present life. Beyond that, all it gives us is a series of

pictures, mostly in the form of visions, of what heaven is like. So actually the question is well-worded. We are told what heaven is 'like' but given no descriptions.

The reason is simple. Heaven is quite literally beyond our comprehension. Can you imagine trying to explain to a caterpillar what it is like to be a butterfly, soaring over the garden? Or to a baby what it is like to play the piano? Heaven is another kind of life, and we have nothing with which to compare it. It is a totally new existence.

So we have to make the best of the pictures that the Bible gives us.

They come in two main varieties. In the Gospels

Most cultures have had their myths of the journey to the next world. The ancient Greeks thought of the ferryman taking them across to the world of the dead.

Jesus constantly spoke of the kingdom of heaven being 'like' this or that: a net, a tree, a field, a pearl of great value. In these 'parables' he was concerned with the principle of God's kingdom, that 'place' where God's will is perfectly done.

We can, of course, experience something of that on earth, as the principles and standards of the kingdom are applied in human life: 'Thy kingdom come, thy will be done on earth, as it is in heaven.'

But heaven is where the kingdom of God reaches its fulfilment, and Jesus' pictures of the kingdom, mentioned above, point to this. The net is pulled in, enclosing all those who are to share in its joys. The field produces its harvest and the time of reaping comes. The precious pearl, bought at great cost, can now be appreciated and enjoyed. The kingdom begins now, as people submit to God's will, but only reaches its fulfilment in heaven.

So the pictures in the parables of Jesus tell us what sort of place heaven is meant to be and the standards that will apply there.

The other pictures of heaven are quite different. They are the amazing, stunning, and at times terrifying, visions written down by John in the last book of the Bible, Revelation. In a series of sweeping impressions—rather like a dream sequence in a film—he is allowed to pull back the curtains and give us a glimpse of 'what shall be hereafter.'

Now the temptation is to treat these visions as though they were literal, like a television documentary of the future. But that is to misunderstand them completely. Terrible confusion has always come to those who insist on treating the book of Revelation in this crude and literal way. It is simply not that sort of a book.

But it is part of the Bible, which Christians regard as inspired by God. It is meant to teach and correct us, to show us truths which are beyond unaided human reason. So we are entitled to look at these pictures with the eyes of faith and to learn what we can from them.

Among those visions is a glorious, beautiful and peaceful picture of heaven, which Revelation calls the 'new Jerusalem', the perfect city of God.

Most people have picked up some ideas from this vision—pearly gates, streets paved with gold, walls of jasper and a sound 'like that of harpists playing their harps'. Again, it's unhelpful to take it all literally. It's a picture of perfection . . . no expense spared, as we say!

When we look at the vision more closely, we see that these gates are never shut. There is no night. Death, mourning, tears and pain have been abolished in this heavenly city. A river of living water flows through the great street, rising from the throne of God and watering the tree of life, whose leaves are 'for the healing of the nations'.

As with all visions, the details are probably unimportant and may even distract us from the true meaning. This is not a picture of what heaven is 'like' in terms of geography, architecture or music. But it is a picture of what heaven is 'like' in a far more important sense—a place of peace, joy, healing and beauty. I doubt if human minds and imaginations are able to go beyond that.

And, incidentally, the picture includes this sentence: 'his servants will serve him.' There will be things to do, and they will form part of God's unending work. We shall not sit on wispy clouds playing harps, but we shall have good, fruitful, satisfying activity. We shall—perfectly, at last—serve him.